Lao-tse · Tao Te King

ZENSHO W. KOPP is one of the most significant western Zen Masters of the present.

He is the direct Dharma successor to Zen Master Soji Enku and the author of a number of books on Zen and Taoism. Zen Master Zensho instructs a large group of students and directs the Tao Chan Zen Center in Wiesbaden, Germany.

The words of the Chinese sage Lao-tse are counted among the inexhaustible sources of eternal wisdom. In a language of incomparable imagery he speaks of the Tao, the divine origin of all existence, and its effect in man as spiritual force.

In radiantly clear aphorisms, like perfectly polished gemstones, the Tao Te King portrays the deep affinity of man with the cosmos. It aims to lead him back to the original oneness with the Tao, and thus into harmony with the all-embracing wholeness of existence, manifest as the unity of all beings.

Lao-tse
Tao Te King

The book of Tao and Spiritual Force

New transcription
with an introduction
by Zensho W. Kopp

Translation © 2014 by John Kitching

Original title: "Tao Te King"
Published by Schirner Verlag Darmstadt 2005

Producer and publisher: Books on Demand GmbH,
Norderstedt

Cover motive: "Lao-tse riding water buffalo"
with kind permission of the religion study collection,
Philipps University, Marburg

Cover design: Michel Schmidt, Jörg Zimmermann
Photo: Verena Kopp
Typesetting: Torsten Zander

Visit our website at
www.tao-chan.org

ISBN: 978-3-84232-861-7

Lao-tse, the Old Master, came into this world when it was his time. When his time was fulfilled he left. Regarding the one who knows of his time and is certain of the fulfilment; coming and going, joy and suffering no longer have power over him.

Chuang-tse (4th. century B.C.)

Contents

Preface

The Tao Te King is one of the most significant and most translated books of world literature and one can hardly imagine today that anyone interested in Eastern religion and philosophy would be unaware of this book.

The words of the Chinese sage Lao-tse are counted among the inexhaustible sources of eternal wisdom. In a language of incomparable imagery he speaks in his Tao Te King of the Tao, the divine origin of all existence, and its spiritual force in man. In radiantly clear aphorisms, like perfectly polished gemstones, the work portrays the deep affinity of man with the cosmos. It aims to lead him back to the original oneness with the Tao, and so into harmony with the all-embracing wholeness of existence, manifest as the unity of all beings.

The version at hand took its impulse from the wish to convey the mystical expressiveness of the Tao Te King, whilst strictly adhering to the original sense, and thus to allow a deeper insight. Furthermore, it was important to me to formulate the work in a clear way which comes as close as possible to the expressive, simple language found in the Chinese original.

In recent times there have been numerous attempts to freely convey the Tao Te King in an everyday, verbose form in order to make it easily understandable. However; all of these are predestined to fail since the Tao Te King is not suitable for such modernisation attempts, regardless of how well-meant they may be.

Every attempt to linguistically smooth out the text and to lengthen it through additions inevitably leads to a falsification of the deeply mystical predications of Lao-tse and draws them down to the level of profanity. Such violations of the text are not only in complete contradiction to the mystical spirit of the Tao Te King but are ultimately extremely embarrassing and make absolutely no sense. To water down the text in such a way, as though it were a product of the modern esoteric wave, means tearing the work from its historic framework and leaving it bereft of its vivacious originality.

As to the language of the Tao Te King, it is arcane, profound, and highly symbolic, so that the work directs itself at the spiritual intuition of the reader. Therefore, its mystical content only reveals itself in its full depth to the inner eye of mystical contemplation. This means that it can only be fully grasped meditatively, beyond logical thinking. Thus by connecting heart and intellect, intuition and logic build the full basis for comprehending the Tao Te King.

And so, whoever takes this book to hand should be aware that its contents cannot be understood solely by means of discriminating, conceptual thought. Consequently, one should not let oneself become discouraged when time is required for a deeper understanding.

The more the reader becomes intimate with the book and reads it with his heart, the more Lao-tse's treasures of oracular wisdom will bear fruit and the Tao Te King will become a friend for life for him.

Wiesbaden, May 2014   Zensho W. Kopp

Introduction

The author of the Tao Te King must seem concealed and mysterious to us, just like the Tao of which he speaks. Chinese tradition has it that Lao-tse was born in the sixth century B.C. in a village called Khü-yen, and seemingly reached a very old age of well over a hundred years. In the "Historical Chronicles" (Chin. Shih-chi) of Szuma Chien, an important Chinese historical work from the first century B.C., it is written:

"Lao-tse, the Old Master, lived in unison with the Tao and its spiritual force. He strove to remain concealed and unremarkable. For a long time he lived in Tschou, but as he saw that Tschou was in the process of decay he mounted a water buffalo and rode off. On arriving at the border pass, he encountered the border guard Yin Hsi, who recognised the master and begged him to leave at least something in writing for future generations.

Thereupon, Lao-tse wrote a book containing over five thousand Chinese characters in which he expressed his thoughts on Tao and its spiritual force. Subsequently, riding on his buffalo, he departed. No one knows where he ended."

Even when the author of the Tao Te King remains concealed from us in the shadows of history, the content and composition of his work bear witness to his personality all the more emphatically. Needless to say, there is no lack of critical voices who endeavour to question the historical existence of the old master or even try to associate him with the realm of myths and legends. However; as early as 1910, the sinologist Richard Wilhelm said of Lao-tse in his commentary on the Tao Te King:

"As with all things historical, the biographical aspect dissolves too for the mystic into meaningless superficiality. And yet, from these aphorisms at hand, an original and inimitable personality speaks to us – in our opinion the best proof of its historicity. But one must have a feeling for such things, one cannot argue over them."

Whilst taking the Tao Te King, literally: "The book of Tao and Spiritual Force", to hand, one will promptly ask oneself: what is Tao?

Western interpreters translate the Chinese symbol "Tao" to: way, being, world-order, sense, reason, track, leader of the universe, just to mention a few. It must be said here, though, that every translation of the word, however well-minded it may be, only illuminates one aspect of the Tao but does not make the Tao itself come alive. For whatever names and circumlocutions we may ascribe to the inconceivable, and thus unspeakable origin of all being, in the end they are but our own limited conceptions and images of the Tao and never the Tao itself. Tao is intangible and indefinable, since defining means setting limits. It is a term for something that eludes all conceptualisation. All attempts to force the Tao into conceptual forms are as if one would attempt to capture heaven in a net. At the very start of the first chapter Lao-tse therefore says:

> The speakable Tao
> is not the eternal Tao.
> The mentionable name
> is not the eternal name.

Furthermore, in the sixth century, the Chinese Zen master Huai Jang said, "Everything that I could tell of it would fall short of the mark."

The true meaning of the Tao is the harmonious transition of nature, the creative base-principle, out of which all things are brought forth, sustained, and dissolved in never ending plenitude. Hence it is the root of all being – unchanging and eternal. It is the absolute, the highest transcendence, the one reality without beginning, from which the universe originates.

The power of the Tao, as it reveals itself in those who live in unison with the Tao is what Lao-tse calls "Te". This he sees as the action of Tao in man. It is what can be called spontaneous experience through Tao.

Although the Chinese word "Te" is sometimes translated as virtue, we should not overlook the fact that it has nothing to do with the conventional term for virtue, as we commonly understand it. For the Taoist, veritable "true virtue" originates from the inner spiritual force in man and is not imposed externally.

Thus, life cannot be pressed into a rigid form by

adhering to regulations. A life based on artificially imposed rules indeed arouses the superficial feeling that all is well, but in fact, it is nothing more than a form of false security.

Te is not the spiritual force of moral rectitude, which by clinging to external moral codes degenerates into a virtue-conscious mentality, to which Lao-tse says:

> High spiritual force is without action,
> therefore it has spiritual force.
> Lesser spiritual force clings to action,
> therefore it has no spiritual force. (38)

The "true spiritual force" originates from an inner spiritual balance which is to be understood as an inner force of the Tao. It is the radiating and merciful power of the Tao, which acts on the surroundings of the wise one, rooted in Tao as pleasant, spontaneous goodness.

The wise one avoids all external form of show since he prefers to remain in seclusion. Peace and tranquillity are of the highest value to him and he endeavours to practise "Wu-wei", "non-action". Now we dare not make the mistake of confusing this non-action with passive, deedless behaviour. Here, Wu-wei means a state of mind of the highest grade of effectiveness, out of which every action is possible at any time. By thus living non-action, the wise one remains in harmony with the Tao, whose universal force bears fruit precisely through his non-intervention. And so, Lao-tse says:

Tao is eternally without action,
but nothing remains undone. (37)

We can see, therefore, that Wu-wei is a matter of creative non-action, an actless conduct which is underlied by the mental attitude of non-intervention, together with the courage of letting things happen.

Wu-wei transcends both extremes – restless activity and absolute inactivity. It is a non-acting of the non-important, which at the same time allows the essential to take effect. This means that in each situation where action is necessary we withdraw ourselves such that the universal effect of the Tao acts through us, so that our whole activity becomes an "acting without action". Lao-tse says:

Practise non-action.
Work without activity. (63)

This means that when we act and at the same time remain in non-action, we practise correct action in unison with the universal law of the Tao. Taoists speak of "flowing together with the Tao". For this reason water is their favourite symbol for the Tao. It represents strength in apparent weakness, it shows us the flow of life and also the adaption to the changing of nature. In its characteristic manner of avoidance and withdrawal, water is at the same time a symbol of non-violence. Therefore, Lao-tse says:

Nothing in the world
is as soft and yielding as water.

And yet it overcomes the hard and strong,
nothing is comparable to it therein. (78)

Water is good,
it aids the myriad beings
and does not quarrel. (8)

For Lao-tse water is the key to the transformation of all things, and only he who knows how to deal with its laws is in harmony with heaven and earth and knows how to act in a correct way. The wise one is aware of how the small and lowly makes life great, and how little is really important considering the impermanence of all things. He sees through the meaninglessness of what the masses believe to be important and worthwhile. Since he does not belong to those who, in their desire for possessions and external stimuli, drift on the surface of existence:

He dwells in inner abundance
and not in outward appearance.
He does not cling to the shell
and lives solely from the essence. (38)

In the Tao Te King; the book of Tao and spiritual force, Lao-tse constantly emphasises how foolish it is to strive for honour, riches and esteem. Wisdom consists in becoming without desires and living modestly in natural simplicity. In the stillness of inner seclusion the wise one experiences his oneness with the Tao, the eternal mother of the universe. As its child, he trusts in its support and security beyond death since:

> He who has found his mother,
> knows himself as her child.
> Knowing himself as her child,
> he remains constantly close to the mother,
> when the body wanes, he is without peril. (52)

Having thus returned to one's true, original nature, one's whole essence resides in harmonious unison with the all-embracing wholeness of existence. It reveals itself in the nature of a bird, which sings out of inner freedom and lives in coessential balance with heaven.

Lao-tse recommends us to follow the way of heaven, to practise non-action and thus let the universal spiritual force of Tao act within us. For heaven is without action but is the cause of all things, literally: "Wei-wu-wei", acting non-action. He who is rooted in Tao and lives in unison with the harmonious movement of heaven becomes a revelation of Tao in the world and attains immortality beyond death.

紫氣東來

Lao-tse riding water buffalo

Taoist painting

Tao Te King

1

The Secret of Tao

The speakable Tao
is not the eternal Tao.
The mentionable name
is not the eternal name.

The nameless
is the beginning of heaven and earth.
The named
is the mother of the myriad beings.

And so:
Constant non-desire
views the most secret.
Constant desire
views only the limited.

These two are of a common origin
and differ only in name.

In their one-being they are a mystery.
The mystery's still deeper mystery
is the gateway to all mysteries.

2

The Emergence of Opposites

When everyone knows: beauty is beautiful,
then ugliness is already there.
When everyone knows: goodness is good,
then evil is already there.

For:
Being and nonbeing create one another.
Difficult and easy determine one another.
Long and short measure one another.
High and low define one another.
Sound and voice complement one another.
Before and after follow one another.

And so the wise one:
He dwells during activity in non-action
and lives the wordless teaching.
The myriad beings appear,
and he does not evade them.

He neither creates nor possesses.
He acts and remains unattached.
When the work is done, he does not linger.

Indeed, only as he does not linger,
does he lose nothing.

3

Contentment through Desirelessness

Not praising the worthy
avoids contention among men.
Not cherishing goods hard to obtain
avoids theft among men.
Not regarding what can be desired
avoids men's hearts to be restive.

And so the wise one rules thus:
He empties their hearts,
steadies their centre,
weakens their desires
and strengthens their character.

He constantly leaves the nation
without knowledge, without desires,
and causes that the wiseacres
do not dare to interfere.

He dwells during activity in non-action
and so everything becomes arranged by itself.

4

The Omnipresence of the Tao

Tao is empty,
but in its action inexhaustible.
A chasm indeed,
it appears as the origin of the myriad beings.

It softens zealousness,
untangles confusions,
mildens glory
and unites with the dust.

Concealed it is, but constantly present.
I do not know whence it comes.
It seems to precede even heaven.

5

Inexhaustible Void

Heaven and earth know no preference.
To them are the myriad beings
like sacrificial straw dogs.
The wise one knows no preference.
To him are the people
like sacrificial straw dogs.

The space between heaven and earth,
is it not comparable to a bellows?
Empty, but inexhaustible,
the more it is moved,
the more comes forth.

Many words melt quickly away,
how much better to preserve the essence.

6

The Valley Spirit

The spirit of the valley is immortal,
it is called the dark feminine.

The gateway of the dark feminine,
it is the origin of heaven and earth.

Eternally lasting, omnipresent
acting without effort.

7

Selflessness

Heaven endures eternally, earth persists.

Heaven and earth can therefore
eternally endure and persist,
as they do not exist for their own sake.
Hence they may eternally endure and persist.

And so the wise one:
He puts his self last
and he progresses forth.
He divests himself of his self
and thus remains preserved himself.

Is it not so, since he is without self-interest?
And so, his innermost achieves completeness.

8

Taoist Values

Supreme goodness is akin to water.

Water is good,
it aids the myriad beings
and does not quarrel.
It inhabits the lowest, which all men despise,
therefore it is close to the Tao.

In dwelling is good: the right base.
In thinking is good: the profoundness.
In giving is good: the love.
In speaking is good: the truth.
In ruling is good: the order.
In acting is good: the ability.
In dealing is good: the timeliness.

But only he, who like water does not quarrel,
remains sacrosanct through this.

9

Baneful Immoderation

To overfill the chalice,
better one would desist.
To oversharpen the knife,
can surely not hold for long.
Is the hall filled with gold and jewels,
then no one can watch over them.
Rich, honoured, and arrogant besides
creates its own misfortune.

To complete the undertaking,
to withdraw oneself,
thus is the heavenly way.

10

Mystical Immersion

Can you unite the powers of your soul,
embrace the One
and in so doing be undivided?
Can you gather the force of your breath,
achieve softness
and in so doing be as a child?
Can you cleanse and sublimate
your inner view
and in so doing be without misapprehension?

Can you love the people,
rule the land
and remain thereby in non-action?
Can you be like a mother bird
when the gates of heaven
open and close?
Can you grasp everything
with radiant clarity
and remain thereby without knowledge?

Create this, nourish this!
Creating, but not possessing.
Acting, but not attaching.
Protecting, but not dominating.

This is called:
profound spiritual force.

11

The Usefulness of the Non-Existent

Thirty spokes surround a nave:
precisely there, where nothing is,
lies the wheel's usefulness.
One shapes clay to form a pot:
precisely there, where nothing is,
lies the pot's usefulness.
One chisels out both door and window,
so that a house emerges:
precisely there, where nothing is,
lies the house's usefulness.

And so:
That which is of essence shows its value
whilst in use only through that which is without essence.

12

Outward Temptation

Resplendent colours blind
the human eye.
Exuberant sounds deafen
the human ear.
Gourmet tastes dull
the human mouth.
Hastening and hounding unsettle
the human heart.
Goods hard to obtain
confound the human condition.

And so the wise one:
He provides for the inner
and not for the outer.

He relinquishes the one and grasps the other.

13

Ego-Free

Favour and disfavour – both are to be feared.
Honour is great suffering like the self.

What does it mean:
favour and disfavour – both are to be feared?

Favour is something lowly.
To gain it is to be feared.
To lose it is to be feared.
That means: favour and disfavour – both are to be feared.

What does it mean:
Honour is great suffering like the self?

That we are plagued by great suffering,
is since we still possess a self.
Were we, however, to achieve selflessness,
would we not also be free from suffering?

And so:
Whoever treasures the world as he does himself,
to him may surely the world be entrusted.
Whoever loves and treats the world as he does himself,
to him may the world be left.

14

Unfathomable Tao

One looks for it and sees it not,
it is called: invisible.
One listens for it and hears it not,
it is called: inaudible.
One reaches for it and grasps it not,
it is called: intangible.

These three, not examinable through reasoning,
interwoven with one another they are one.

Its upper is not light,
its lower is not dark.
Ceaselessly onwards it flows,
endless, nameless,
and returns to the being-less.

That is: of the formless form,
of the imageless image.
That is: the most unfathomable of the unfathomable.

One approaches it and sees not its beginning.
One follows it and sees not its end.

When the Tao of the forefathers is preserved,
to guide the essence of today,
from time immortal one can Know.
This is called: endless unfolding of the Tao.

15

The Masters of Old

The veritable masters of old
were subtle, arcane and profound.
Concealed they were, and inscrutable.
Since inscrutable,
I can describe them only with difficulty.

Heedful they were,
like he who crosses a river in winter,
cautious, like he who fears the surrounding neigh-
bours,
reticent like a visiting guest,
yielding like melting ice,
simple like unhewn wood,
far reaching like the valley,
inscrutable like turbid water.

Who can, through tranquillity,
gradually clear the turbidness?
Who can, through motion,
gradually enliven the tranquillity?

He who preserves this Tao
does not seek other plenitude.
But only he who does not seek other plenitude
cannot be blinded by innovation,
he can be lowly
and attain completeness.

16

Perceiving the Eternal

Reach the utmost emptiness,
enshrine the steadfast silence.
The countless forms unfold,
but I watch how they turn back again.

The beings blossom, resplendent and colourful,
but return home to the basal root.

Returning to the root means: stillness.
Stillness means: returning to destiny.
Returning to destiny means: eternity.
Perceiving the eternal means: enlightenment.

Non-perception of the eternal, however,
brings baneful disarray.

He who perceives the eternal is all-embracing.
The all-embracing one is righteous unto all.
The righteous one is regal.
The regal one is of heavenly kind.
The heavenly one is united with the Tao.

He who is united with Tao can eternally abide.
When the body wanes, he remains without peril.

17

Hidden Ruler

Of a great ruler
the people only know: he exists.
A less greater they love and praise.
A still less greater they fear.
A still less greater they despise.

He who does not trust enough
cannot be trusted.

The true ruler brings forth few words.

Is his work complete, the deed accomplished,
the people say:
"It happened as if by itself."

18

The Loss of Tao

When the great Tao goes adrift,
benefaction and rectitude arise.
When knowledge and cleverness appear,
great hypocrisy follows.

When the family harmony shatters,
filial duty and parental devotion arise.
Is the land caught in confusion,
there are always the faithful public servants.

19

Returning to Simplicity

Give up sanctity,
throw off cleverness,
and the people will gain a hundredfold.
Give up benefaction,
throw off rectitude,
and the people will find natural love.
Give up cunningness,
throw off avarice,
and no more will there be robbers and thieves.

These three are but pleasant illusion,
and so can never suffice.

And so:
Preserve purity,
manifest simplicity,
diminish selfishness,
abate avidity!

20

Different from the Others

He who ceases all learning has no troubles.

The hesitant "yes" and the willing "yes",
is there a difference?
But good and evil,
is there no difference?

What others esteem, that too I should honour.
What nonsense!
Oh, what confusion in this world,
and without end!

People are all so joyous
as when celebrating great festivals,
as when climbing the terraces in spring.

I alone remain silent and unmoved
like a new-born child who has yet to laugh;
unattached, independent.

The masses have their opulence,
only I alone seem to possess nothing.
My heart is that of a fool's;
shrouded, inscrutable.

People are all so bright and clear,
only I am turbid and dark.
People are all so clever and astute,
only I am foolish and simple-minded.

I drift along like the sea,
without direction, like the restless wind.
People all have a purpose,
only I am a useless fool.

I alone am different from the others
but I revere the nourishing mother.

21

The Origin of all Things

The motion of highest spiritual force
only ever follows the Tao.

The action of the Tao –
so intangible, so eluding.

Eluding, intangible,
it embodies all images.
Intangible, eluding,
it embodies all forms.
Dark, unfathomable,
it embodies the life-force.

The life-force is reality,
its innermost highest certitude.

From the very beginning till today
its name does not wane.
It engenders the origination of all things.

How I know of the origination of all things?
Indeed, through this, the Tao.

22

Harmonic Balance

The imperfect becomes perfect.
The twisted becomes straight.
The unfilled becomes filled.
The old becomes new.
The little becomes much.
Too much brings confusion.

And so the wise one:
Embracing the One,
he becomes an example to the world.
He does not flaunt himself,
thus he shines.
He does not assert himself,
thus he is respected.
He does not praise himself,
thus he has merit.
He does not elevate himself,
thus he stands out.

Since he does not quarrel,
no one can quarrel with him.

Like the elders did proclaim:
"The imperfect becomes perfect",
and are those empty words?

All flows to him who is truly sublime.

23

Becoming One with Tao

Sparsity of speech is in accordance with nature.

A hurricane does not last a whole morning.
A downpour does not last a whole day.
But who brings forth wind and rain?
Heaven and earth.

But if heaven and earth
are unable to provide permanence,
how much less then can man?

And so:
He who follows the Tao
will become one with the Tao.
He who follows the highest spiritual force
will become one with the highest spiritual force.
He who has lost it
will become one with his loss.

He at one with the Tao
will be willingly embraced by the Tao.
He at one with the highest spiritual force
will be willingly embraced by the highest spiritual
force.
He at one with its loss
will be willingly embraced by the loss.

He who does not trust enough
cannot be trusted.

24

Craving for Recognition

He who stands on tiptoe
does not stand firmly.
He who walks splay-legged
makes no progress.
He who flaunts himself
does not shine.
He who asserts himself
is not respected.
He who praises himself
has no merit.
He who elevates himself
does not stand out.

From the perspective of the Tao this is called:
refuse and abnormal outgrowths,
and this arouses repugnance in all beings.

And so:
He who follows the Tao does not behave so.

25

Intangible Tao

There is a being, intangible, sublime.
It precedes heaven and earth,
so silent, so formless.
Alone in itself, unchanging,
all-pervading, ever-present.
It can be called the mother of the universe.

I do not know its name,
I call it: Tao.

When I strive to define it,
I call it: great.
Great, that is, eternally flowing.
Eternally flowing, that is, endless vastness.
Endless vastness, that is, ceaselessly returning.

And so:
Great is Tao.
Great is heaven.
Great is earth.
Great too is the majestical.
Four grandeurs there are in the world,
the majestical is one of them.

Man follows the earth.
The earth follows heaven.
Heaven follows the Tao.
The Tao follows itself.

26

Conscientiousness

Heavy is the root of light.
Calm is the master of unrest.

And so the wise one:
Even when travelling the whole day,
he does not carelessly part from his luggage.
Even when surrounded by interesting things,
he remains serene and unmoved.

What, however, if a great ruler
acts frivolously with the realm
for his own gain?

Through frivolity he loses the root.
Through unrest he loses the leadership.

27

Well-Kept

A good traveller follows neither track nor trail.
A good speaker does not speak affectedly.
A good arithmetician needs no abacus.
A good door needs no bolt,
but no one can open it.
That which is well tied does not constrict,
but no one can undo it.

And so the wise one:
He always knows how to keep the people,
since he rejects no one.
He always knows how to keep the beings,
since he rejects none of the beings.
This is called: following the light.

And so:
Be the good man the bad man's teacher,
be the bad man the good man's pupil.

To not honour one's teacher,
to not love one's pupil,
despite all knowledge, it would be great ignorance.

This is a great secret.

28

The Unison of Yin and Yang

Know the masculine, preserve the feminine,
thus you become the riverbed of the world.
Being the riverbed of the world,
highest spiritual force does not leave you,
and you return home to innocence.

Know the light, preserve the dark,
thus you become an example to the world.
Being an example to the world,
you do not lack highest spiritual force,
and you return home to boundlessness.

Know inner greatness, preserve humility,
thus you become the valley of the world.
Being the valley of the world,
you have the fullness of highest spiritual force,
and return home to naturalness.

Is naturalness divided,
there are then the valuable people.
When the wise one makes use of naturalness,
he becomes a leader of the people.

And so:
The truly great is undivided.

29

The Wisdom of Non-Interfering

Should one desire to seize the world
in order to change it,
I see in advance that it will founder.

The world is a spiritual entity,
one must not influence it.
He who influences it destroys it,
he who seizes it loses it.

And so the beings:
Sometimes they lead,
other times they follow.
Sometimes they breathe warmly,
other times they gasp coldly.
Sometimes they are strong,
other times they are weak.
Sometimes they climb high,
other times they plunge deep.

And so the wise one:
He avoids the all-too often.
He avoids the all-too much.
He avoids the all-too large.

30

Victory Without Use of Force

He who with Tao besteads a ruler
does not enslave the world with force of arms.
His actions could return on him.

Where armies have camped
thornbushes and thistles grow.
After a great war great hardship follows.

The good man seeks only victory and nothing more,
after conquest he is not violent.

He wins and does not triumph.
He wins and does not praise himself.
He wins and is not arrogant.
He wins and is not violent.
He wins only when there is no alternative.

That which has grown too strong will decay.
That means: being without Tao.
That without Tao soon perishes.

31

Disastrous Weapons

Even the most magnificent weapons
are tools of disaster,
they are abhorred by the beings.
Therefore, he who has Tao turns away from them.

The noble one in his house prizes the left,
when he controls the weapons, he prizes the right.

Weapons are tools of disaster
and no tools of the noble one;
but if unavoidable, he makes use of them.

Peace and tranquillity are of the foremost to him.

He wins but does not rejoice in it.
Were he to rejoice, it would be joy in murder.

If one has joy in murder,
never will he attain life's aim.

On cheerful occasions the place of honour
is to the left.
On sorrowful occasions the place of honour
is to the right.

In the army the sub-commander stands to the left,
the chief commander stands to the right.
That signifies:

He stands as though at a funeral service.

People killed in great numbers,
with great anguish it should be lamented.
He who wins in battle
should stand as though at a funeral service.

32

Natural Order

Tao is eternal and nameless.
Although so simple,
the world is unable to grasp it.

If princes and kings
were able to preserve it,
the myriad things
would flow to them as though of their own accord.

Heaven and earth would unite,
to send down blessings of dew.
People without law and order
would gain order as though of their own accord.

When the regulation begins, names arise.
Once names are there,
so must one know how to stop.
He who knows how to stop comes not into danger.

Tao's existence in the world:
It is like the sea,
into which all streams and rivers flow.

33

Preserving the Centre

He who knows others is clever;
he who knows himself is wise.
He who subjugates others is strong;
he who subjugates himself is undefeatable.
He who asserts himself is strong-willed;
he who is contented is rich.

He who does not lose his centre has durability.
He who does not even perish in death lives eternally.

34

All-Permeating Tao

All-permeating is the Tao,
in every direction present.

The myriad beings owe it their lives,
and it does not desert them.
It completes its work
and does not call it its own.

It clothes and nourishes the myriad beings
and does not make itself master.
Since eternally without desire,
it can be called small.

The myriad beings turn to it,
and it does not make itself master,
so can it be called great.

It never makes itself great,
and so it may fulfil great things.

35

The Great Archetype

He who abides by the great archetype,
to him the world will come.
It comes, there is no suffering,
only tranquillity, peace, and bliss.

For music and delicious dishes
the passing traveller stops,
but should one speak of Tao,
he finds no taste for it.

He who looks for it
sees nothing special.
He who listens for it
hears nothing special.
He who draws strength from it
finds no end to it.

36

Clear Perception of the Concealed

That which one wishes to compress,
must first properly expand.
That which one wishes to weaken,
must first properly become strong.
That which one wishes to dispose of,
must first properly flourish.
Where one wishes to take,
one must first properly give.

This is called:
clear perception of the concealed.

The soft subjugates the hard.
The weak subjugates the strong.

Never may the fish leave the water's depths.
The land's most effective weapons
must not be shown to the people.

37

The Effect of Non-Action

Tao is eternally without action,
but nothing remains undone.

Princes and kings,
if they could retain this,
the myriad beings
would transform of their own accord.
Were they to transform, however,
and still desired to act,
I would know how to restrain them:
through nameless simplicity.

Nameless simplicity
well, it leads to freedom from desire.
Freedom from desire, however, leads to stillness,
and so the world organises itself of its own accord.

38

Intentionless Spiritual Force

High spiritual force is without action,
therefore it has spiritual force.
Lesser spiritual force clings to action,
therefore it has no spiritual force.

High spiritual force is non-action,
it acts solely without intention.
Lesser spiritual force is action,
and thereby acts with intention.

High humanity acts,
it acts solely without intention.
High rectitude acts
and thereby acts with intention.
High morality acts,
and if one does not follow
it stretches forth its arm and forces it.

Therefore:
If Tao is lost,
lesser spiritual force will remain.
If lesser spiritual force is lost,
humanity will remain.
If humanity is lost,
rectitude will remain.
If rectitude is lost,
morality will remain.

Morality, however,
is only the outward appearance of faithfulness and
belief and the beginning of all disarray.
Extrinsic knowledge is only a limp blossom of the
Tao and the beginning of all folly.

And so the truly great one:
He dwells in inner abundance
and not in outward appearance.
He does not cling to the shell
and lives solely from the essence.

And so:
Relinquish the one and grasp the other!

39

Fundamental Tao

From of old these obtained the One:

Heaven received the One and became clear.
Earth received the One and became firm.
The gods received the One and became mighty.
The river valleys received the One and became full.
The myriad beings received the One
and became animate.
Princes and kings received the One
and became a guide to the world.

The One engendered all this.

Heaven without that through which it became clear,
would certainly collapse.
Earth without that through which it became firm,
would certainly decay.
The gods without that through which they became
mighty,
would certainly pass away.
The river valleys without that through which they
became full,
would certainly dry up.
The beings without that through which they live,
would certainly perish.
The princes and kings without that
through which they became noble and exalted,
would certainly be overthrown.

And so:
Noble has lowly as its root,
Elevated has ignoble as its base.

Therefore, princes and kings also call themselves
orphaned, lonely, insignificant.
And do they not do so
since they make being lowly their root?

And so:
He who overly seeks honour
remains without honour.

Do not wish to shine like a jewel,
but then to fall like a stone.

40

The Motion of Tao

Returning is the motion of the Tao.
Softness is the active force of the Tao.

The myriad beings arise from oneness.
Oneness arises from nothingness.

41

True Perfection

When one of great insight hears of Tao,
he follows it and lives according to it.
When one of average insight hears of Tao,
he half believes it and half doubts it.
When one without insight hears of Tao,
he laughs loudly about it.
If he does not laugh, it was not true Tao.

And so was said by those of old:
He enlightened in Tao appears benighted.
He who strides ahead in Tao appears left behind.
He who is well-balanced in Tao appears boorish.

Highest spiritual force appears like the deep valley.
Great purity appears as though besmirched.
Far-reaching spiritual force appears as though tight-
ly confined.
Strong spiritual force appears as though weak.
True perfection appears as though imperfect.

The great square is without corners.
The great fulfilment takes time to reach maturity.
The great sound rings out most softly.
The great image has no form.

Tao is concealed and nameless,
but it nourishes all beings and completes them.

42

Harmony of Yin and Yang

Tao gives rise to the One,
the One gives rise to the Two,
the Two give rise to the Three,
the Three give rise to the myriad beings.

The myriad beings,
the dark Yin, it sustains them,
the bright Yang embraces them.
The all-encompassing life's breath
brings forth their harmonious accord.

That which people abhor,
is to be orphaned, lonely, and insignificant,
but princes and kings
make it their self-designation.

And so the beings:
Sometimes they diminish
and in so doing increase.
Sometimes they increase
and in so doing diminish.

What others teach, I also teach:
The hard and strong does not die a good death.
I shall make this the principle of my teachings.

43

The Power of Non-Action

The softest of all in the world
subjugates the hardest of all in the world.
The non-being penetrates
the seamlessly impenetrable.

By this I recognise
the value of non-action.

Teaching without words,
remaining in non-action during activity,
only few achieve this in the world.

44

Steadfastness through Contentedness

Glory or life: which means more?
Life or riches: which is more valuable?
Gain or loss: which is worse?

Therefore:
He who sets his heart on much
will waste himself severely.
Much hoarding of possessions
will turn to his loss.

He who knows how to be contented
does not come into disgrace.
He who knows how to stop
does not come into danger,
and so he can last long.

45

Great Perfection

Great perfection is like inadequacy,
but in its action immortal.
Great plenitude is like emptiness,
but whilst in use provides endlessly.

Great straightness is like crookedness.
Great wisdom is like foolishness.
Great speech is like silentness.

Motion overcomes coldness.
Tranquillity overcomes heat.

Clarity and tranquillity
give the right measure back to the world.

46

Disastrous Desiring

When Tao rules in the world,
the steed draws manure over the field.
When Tao does not rule in the world,
the war-horses graze the fields.

No malady is greater,
than to cherish many desires.
No disaster is greater,
than to not know contentment.
No error is greater,
than to desire possessions.

Therefore:
He who knows to be contented with what suffices
will always have enough.

47

Inner Perception

Without leaving the house,
one can understand the whole world.
Without looking through the window,
one can see the Tao of heaven.

The further one goes out,
the less one knows.

And so the wise one:
Without travelling forth, he comprehends.
Without looking, he perceives.
Without acting, he brings to completion.

48

Dwelling in Non-Action

He who devotes himself to learning
increases daily.
He who devotes himself to the Tao
decreases daily.
Decreases, and decreases again
and thus comes to non-action.

Abiding in non-action
nothing remains undone.

If one wants to gain the world,
so be he constantly free from bustling activity.
If one is much occupied,
he is not suitable to gain the world.

The Open Heart

The wise one does not have a closed heart,
to him, the people's hearts
are his own heart.

To good people I am good,
to bad people I am also good.
True spiritual force is goodness.

To sincere people I am sincere,
to insincere people I am also sincere.
True spiritual force is sincerity.

The wise one lives quietly in the world,
his heart is an open space.
People see and hear him,
and in all of them he sees his children.

50

Beyond Death

Going out into life is entering into death.

Three from ten rise to life.
Three from ten aspire to death.
Three from ten come into distress,
since they drive themselves to death.

Why is that so?
Since they live life's excesses.

And so I have heard:
He who knows well to preserve life
wanders though the land
and does not flee from rhinoceros and tiger.
He strides through an army
and carries no armour and weapons.
The rhinoceros finds nothing
to thrust its horn into.
The tiger finds nothing
to sink its claws into.
The weapon finds nothing
to gouge its tip into.

Why is that so?
Since he is beyond death.

51

Profound Spiritual Force

Tao engenders.
Its spiritual force nourishes.
Its essence forms.
Its might accomplishes.

Therefore the myriad beings revere the Tao
and prize its spiritual force.
Tao is revered and its spiritual force is prized,
since it never compels,
and so the forms grow and flourish of their own accord.

For:
Tao engenders them,
its spiritual force nourishes them,
lets them grow and flourish,
lets them mature and reach completion.

Creating but not possessing
acting, but not attaching
protecting, but not dominating.

This is called:
profound spiritual force.

52

Uniting with the Eternal

It was a beginning of the universe,
this is the mother of the myriad beings.

He who has found his mother
knows himself as her child.
Knowing himself as her child,
he remains constantly close to the mother,
when his body wanes, he is without peril.

One should curb one's urge to speak
and close the gates of one's senses,
when the body wanes, he remains without concern.

If one does not curb one's urge to speak
and is constantly occupied,
when the body wanes, he is without salvation.

To perceive the smallest means: enlightenment.
To preserve softness means: strength.

If one makes use of his inner light
to find back to enlightenment,
he will not decease at the body's destruction.

This is called:
uniting oneself with the eternal.

53

Fallacious Ways

He who has once perceived
abides constantly in the great Tao,
and his only fear will be to deviate from it.

The sublime way is very simple,
but people love indirect ways.

When the palaces are pompously decorated,
the fields are full of weeds
and the barns are empty.
The nobilities dress in resplendent robes
and carry the finely-honed sword.
They fill themselves with drink and fare
and possess treasures and goods to excess.

But I call this:
deplorable ostentation of robbers and thieves.

That means: being without Tao.

54

All-Embracing Spiritual Force

That which is well-founded has constancy.
That which is well-protected does not go astray.
Thus it is cherished
from generation to generation.

If cultivated this, for oneself only,
veritable the spiritual force will be.
If cultivated this in one's house,
spiritual force flows abundantly forth.
If cultivated this at one's place,
spiritual force grows onward with strength.
If cultivated this in the whole land,
spiritual force blossoms without respite.
If cultivated this in the world as a whole,
spiritual force encompasses all.

And so:
According to this self judge the self of others.
According to this house judge the house of others.
According to this place judge the place of others.
According to this land judge the land of others.
According to this world judge the world of others.

How do I know that it is so in the world?
Indeed through this, the Tao.

Living in Unison

He who has the fullness of spiritual force within him
is like a newborn child.

Poisonous insects do not sting it,
wild animals do not claw it
and birds of prey do not snatch it.
Its bones are weak, its tendons soft,
but its grip is firm.
It is yet to know of man and woman,
but within it the plenitude of the life-force stirs.
Even if it screams the whole day,
it does not become hoarse.
This is perfect unison.

Perceiving unison means: being eternal.
Perceiving the eternal means: enlightenment.

Living in excess, I call
evoking disaster.
Using one's life-force according to one's desires,
I call, becoming strong and rigid.

That which has become too strong decays.
That means: being without Tao.
That without Tao soon perishes.

56

Concealed Unification

He who knows does not speak.
He who speaks does not know.

Curb your urge to speak,
close the gates of your senses,
soften your zealousness,
untangle your confusions,
milden your glory,
and unite with the dust of the earth.

This is called: concealed unification.

He who has achieved this
is neither moved by affection
nor aversion,
is neither moved by gain
nor loss,
is neither moved by prestige
nor disdain.

And so he is the noblest of the world.

Concealed Effect

With justness one rules a land.
With cunning one makes war.
Free from bustling activity one gains the world.

How I know that it is so?

Through this:
The more there are restrictions and prohibitions,
the poorer the people become.
The more sharp weapons people have,
the more confusion is in the world.
The more dexterity and cleverness people have,
the more strange things arise.
The more there are laws and decrees enacted,
the more there are robbers and thieves.

And so the wise one says:
I cultivate non-action,
and the people change of their own accord.
I cultivate tranquillity,
and the people become righteous of their own accord.
I cultivate being without bustling activity,
and the people gain sufficiency of their own accord.
I cultivate contentedness,
and the people gain simplicity of their own accord.

58

Order without Regulation

If the government is calm and reticent,
the people are simple and modest.
If the government is zealous and strict,
the people are malicious and corrupt.

In misfortune good fortune is concealed.
In good fortune misfortune is concealed.
But who knows how it will end?
Is one not able to arrange it?

But the order turns to disorder,
goodness turns to hypocrisy,
and the people's ignorance
increases from day to day.

And so the wise one:
He is an example, without curtailing.
He is sincere, without harming.
He is just, without imposing.
He shines, without blinding.

59

Well-Founded in Tao

When one leads the people and serves heaven,
nothing is better than modesty.

For only through modesty
will one obey the Tao in good time.
If one obeys the Tao in good time,
one amply increases the fullness of spiritual force.

If one amply increases the fullness of spiritual force,
nothing is impossible to him.
If nothing is impossible to him,
then no one can know his limits.
He whose limits no one knows
may possess the world.

If one possesses the eternal mother of the world,
one can persist eternally.
I call this: deeply rooted and well-founded in Tao.

This means:
eternal life and endless contemplation.

60

Ruling the Land with Tao

One must rule a great land heedfully,
as when one fries small fish.

If one rules the world with Tao,
evil forces will not rise up.
Not that evil no longer has any power,
but its power does not harm people.
Not just its power does not harm people,
also the wise one does not harm people.

Now, since they both do not harm,
spiritual force flows forth and unites them.

61

Remaining Lowly

A great land
should be like a river's lowland plain,
and so become a reservoir to the world,
the feminine of the world.

Steadfastly the feminine overcomes
the masculine through its tranquillity.
Through tranquillity it keeps itself lowly.

Therefore the great land,
it places itself beneath the small land
and in so doing wins the small land.
The small land,
it places itself beneath the great land
and in so doing wins the great land.

And so:
The one places itself beneath in order to win,
the other places itself beneath in order to be won.

The great land should desire nothing more
than to embrace the other and to nourish it.
The small land should desire nothing more
than to join the other and to serve it.

Thus both achieve what they aim,
but the great one must hold itself lowly.

62

Precious Tao

Tao is refuge to the myriad beings,
the highest treasure of good men,
the last salvation of bad men.

With pleasant words one can bargain for honour.
With fine manners one can gain prestige.

But those in the populace lacking goodness,
why should one reject them?

For this, the emperor was enthroned
and the three highest ministers appointed.
Even when they hold high jade tablets
and thus precede the four-horse drawn carriage,
it would nonetheless be better
to sit still and follow the Tao.

What was the reason
that those of old did thus revere this Tao?
Did they not say:
he who seeks shall find,
he who is guilty shall be forgiven?

Therefore it is the most precious of the world.

63

Recognising the Great in the Small

Practise non-action.
Work without activity.
Taste without savouring.
Recognise the great in the small
and the many in the few.

Repay injustice with goodness.

Plan that which is difficult while it is easy.
Do that which is great while it is small.

The difficult things in the world
always begin with the easy things.
The greatest things in the world
always begin with the small things.

And so the wise one:
He never begins with the great,
therefore he may achieve great deeds.

He who promises lightly seldom keeps his word.
He who takes many things too lightly
gathers many troubles.

And so the wise one:
Since he takes nothing lightly,
he remains without troubles.

Heeding Beginning and End

That which is still at rest is easy to keep.
That which has yet to reveal itself is easy to avert.
That which is still tender is easy to break.
That which is still fine is easy to scatter.

Act, before things appear.
Regulate, before confusion begins.

A tree of mighty girth
originates from a tiny shoot.
A pagoda nine stories high
rises aloft from a heap of earth.
A journey of a thousand miles
begins with the first step.

He who acts ruins it.
He who seizes loses it.

And so the wise one:
He dwells in non-action,
therefore he ruins nothing.
He does not aim to seize,
therefore he loses nothing.

When people undertake a deed,
they often ruin it just before completion.
Yet, if one heeds the end as he does the beginning,
it cannot be ruined.

And so the wise one:
He wishes to be without desires,
and does not cherish scarcely attainable goods.
He learns not to learn,
and turns to that
which the masses pass by.

Thus he fosters the natural course of the myriad beings,
but does not dare to interfere.

65

Dangerous Cleverness

Those of old who followed the Tao,
did not enlighten the people thereby.
They wanted to keep them in simpleness.
Difficult it is to rule the people
if their cleverness is too great.

Therefore:
To rule the land with cleverness,
brings disaster to the land.
To not rule the land with cleverness,
brings fortune to the land.

He who recognises these both
has a well-tried model.
Enduring knowledge of this well-tried model
is called: profound spiritual force.

Profound spiritual force
is concealed and far-reaching
and in contradiction to the beings.
But it leads back again to the great unison.

66

The Power of Humbleness

Rivers and seas,
through what are they able
to be kings of the myriad streams?

Since they are admirable in being lowly,
they can be kings of the myriad streams.

And so the wise one:
If he wishes to be higher than the people,
he must humbly keep himself low.
If he wishes to precede the people
he must place himself last.

Thus the wise one:
He abides above
and does not burden the people.
He abides ahead
and does not harm the people.
Joyously, the world supports him
and does not become weary of him.

Since he quarrels with no one,
no one can quarrel with him.

Three Gems

The whole world says my path is indeed great,
but it is abnormal.
Precisely because it is great it is abnormal.
Were it not to be abnormal,
it would be insignificant.

I possess three gems, which I treasure and protect.
The first is called: love, the second is called: modesty,
and the third: to not dare to be ahead in the world.

Through love one can be fearless.
Through modesty one can be generous.
If one does not dare to be ahead in the world,
one can be foremost among people.

Nowadays, one spurns love
and is courageous besides,
one spurns modesty
and is wasteful besides,
one spurns standing back
and pushes forwards besides.
This is doomed to death.

If one has love in battle, he will prevail,
if one has it when defending, he is invincible.

He who heaven wishes to preserve
is protected by love.

68

The Spiritual Force of Non-Dispute

A good commander is not warlike.
A good fighter does not become enraged.
A good conqueror of enemies does not oppress.
A good leader of men keeps himself low.

That is the spiritual force of non-dispute,
that is the strength of leadership of men.

This is called:
being in unison with heaven,
the highest aim of those of old.

69

He Who Retreats Wins

There is a saying when using weapons:

I do not dare to play master,
but rather bide my time like a guest.
I do not dare to advance one inch,
but rather retreat one foot.

That means:
To move forth without moving oneself.
To ward off without lifting one's arms.
To throw back without attacking.
To conquer without weapons.

No disaster is greater
than to underestimate the enemy.
To underestimate the enemy
is almost the loss of our possessions.

Therefore:
Wherever there is a call to arms,
he who retreats will always win.

70

Rare Understanding

My words are very easy to understand,
very easy to heed.
Yet no one in the world can understand them,
no one can heed them.

My words have a creator,
my works have a master.
But only since one cannot understand him
am I also not understood.

Those who understand me are rare,
consequently, I am revered.

And so the wise one:
He wears an inconspicuous robe
and holds the jewel in his heart.

71

Knowing One's Ignorance

Knowing of one's ignorance is greatness.
Not knowing of one's ignorance is suffering.
Yet only he who recognises this suffering as suffering
will thus become free from suffering.

The wise one does not suffer
for he has recognised this suffering as suffering.
Therefore he is free from suffering.

72

The Virtue of Power

If people do not fear power,
it will become virtuous.

Do not confine their living space
nor make their lives toilsome.
Only when you do not make their lives toilsome
will they not grow weary of you.

And so the wise one:
He knows himself,
but does not show it.
He loves himself,
but is not presumptuous.

And so:
He relinquishes the one and grasps the other.

73

The Tao of Heaven

The courage to take risks
leads to death.
The courage to not take risks
preserves life.
These two, sometimes they can be useful,
other times they can be harmful.

Of the one who has heaven's wrath,
who knows the reason why?

And so the wise one remains circumspect.

The Tao of heaven:
It does not contend
yet knows well how to overcome.
It does not speak
yet knows well how to give answer.
It does not call
yet everything comes of its own accord.
Patient it is
yet acts when the time is right.

Heaven's net is infinitely wide
and its mesh is great,
but nothing escapes it.

74

Power Over Life and Death

If people do not fear death,
how can one then affright them with death?

But supposing people would constantly fear death,
and one could seize and execute the one
who does abhorrent deeds – who would then dare
to do this?

One power only decides over life and death.
To kill in place of this power would mean,
to wield the axe in place of the great carpenter.

But if one wields the axe
in place of the great carpenter,
he will certainly injure his hand.

75

The Rulers' Voracity

People starve
because the rulers devour too many taxes,
therefore they starve.
People are hard to lead
because the rulers interfere,
therefore they are hard to lead.
People take death too lightly,
because the rulers cling to life too much,
therefore they take death too lightly.

Yet only he who does not clutch at life,
is wiser than he who lives wantonly.

The Hard and the Soft

Man enters into life
soft and weak
and dies hard and rigid.

Grasses and trees enter into life
yielding and tender
and die parched and withered.

Therefore:
The hard and rigid accompanies death.
The soft and weak accompanies life.

And so:
If the armies are strong and rigid,
they will not prevail.
If the trees are strong and rigid,
they will be felled.

The hard and strong ebbs.
The soft and weak ascends.

Being in Balance

The Tao of heaven
how comparable it is to drawing a bow!

That which is high is pulled down,
that which is low is lifted up.
That which is excessive is abated,
that which is insufficient is completed.

The Tao of heaven:
it abates the excessive
and completes the insufficient.

Not so the people's way:
they reduce that which is insufficient,
to present it to those who already live in excess.

Who, however, can use his excess
to present it to the world?
Only he who has Tao.

And so the wise one:
He acts but remains unattached.
When the work is done he does not linger.
He does not wish to show his wisdom.

78

The Weak Overcomes the Strong

Nothing in the world
is as soft and yielding as water.
And yet it overcomes the hard and strong,
nothing is comparable to it therein.
This it can do easily through what it is not.

The weak overcomes the strong,
the soft overcomes the hard.

There is no one in the world to whom it is unknown,
but it is applied by no one.

And so the wise one says:
He who takes on the dishonour in the land
shall be acknowledged as a holy man.
He who besides takes on hardship and pain
the rank of king in his land may he gain.

True words are like reversed.

Duty and Demands

If one reconciles great resentment,
residual resentment will still remain.
How can this be made up?

And so the wise one:
He keeps only to his duty
and does not demand anything of others.

He who has spiritual force,
keeps to his duty.
He who has no spiritual force,
keeps to his demands.

The Tao of heaven makes no preferences,
eternally it gives to him who proves himself as good.

80

Taoist Life

A land may be small, its inhabitants few.

Let it have a hundred and one devices
and not make use of them.
Let the people take death seriously
and not travel far afield.
Let it have ships and carriages
but no reason to mount them.
Let it have armour and weapons
but no reason to apply them.
Let the people once again knot cords
and make use of them.

Flavoursome be their fare,
beautiful their clothes,
peaceful their dwellings
and joyous their customs.

Neighbouring countries may lie close together,
so that cocks and dogs can be heard at a distance,
and yet, one reaches old age and death,
without having travelled to and fro.

81

True Words

True words are not pleasant,
pleasant words are not true.

The good man does not speak pleasingly,
he who speaks pleasingly is not good.
The wise one is not learned,
the scholar is not wise.

The wise one does not amass possessions,
the more he does for others,
the more he possesses.
The more he gives to others,
the more he receives.

The Tao of heaven is:
helping without harming.
The Tao of the wise one is:
acting without contending.

Contact

ZEN-ZENTRUM
TAO 道禅 CHAN

Tao Chan Zentrum e.V.
Gemeinnütziger Verein
Adelheidstr. 37
D-65195 Wiesbaden
Germany

The Tao Chan Zen Center is under the personal direction of Zen-Master Zensho W. Kopp.
During his many years as an active spiritual master, a large community of students has come together whom he regularly instructs.

Zen-Sesshin
Twice a month, Zen Master Zensho leads a Zen-day where guests may participate.

Information and registration
Tel. +49 (0)611 940 623 -1 Fax -2
www.tao-chan.org
www.facebook.com/ZenZentrumTaoChan

Books by Zensho W. Kopp

Words of the Awakened Mind

Aphorisms of a Western Zen Master

120 pages, paperback, 9.95 €
Books on Demand GmbH
ISBN 978-3-8482-4134-7
Original title: Worte eines Erwachten

LOOK INSIDE!

The Freedom of Zen

The Zen book that shatters all limits and bounds

216 pages, paperback, 12.95 €
Books on Demand GmbH
ISBN 978-3-8391-6893-6
Original title: Die Freiheit des Zen

LOOK INSIDE!

All English books available at: **www.tao-chan.org**

MUSIC BY ZENSHO W. KOPP

Satori

The Great Liberation –
Electronic symphonies
of a Zen Master

1 CD, 55 min., 12.99 €
Amazon Publishing
ASIN: 887936949722

LISTEN NOW!

MUSIC CD

Transformation

Mystical Sound Dimensions

1 CD, 48 min., 12.99 €
Amazon Publishing
ASIN: B00H4H0NVS

LISTEN NOW!

MUSIC CD

All music cds available at: **www.tao-chan.org**

ARTWORK BY ZENSHO W. KOPP

Enlightened Dimensions of the Divine

Paintings and quotations of a Western Zen Master

140 pages, 60 colour plates, 16.99 €
Amazon Publishing
ISBN 978-1-4827-9942-2

Also available in French and Spanish
Original title: Im Farbenrausch des Göttlichen

LOOK INSIDE!

Available at: **www.tao-chan.org**